How Does
Echolocation
Work?

by Laura Johnson

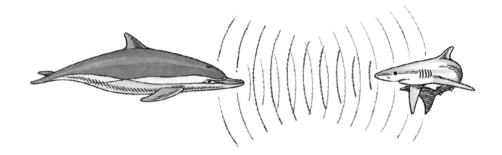

Scott Foresman
is an imprint of

Glenview, Illinois • Boston, Massachusetts • Chandler, Arizona
Upper Saddle River, New Jersey

ISBN 13: 978-0-328-51662-9
ISBN 10:   0-328-51662-7

2 3 4 5 6 7 8 9 10 V0B4 18 17 16

Human Ears

What body parts do people and animals use to hear? If you answered *ears*, you would be correct about people and most animals—but not all animals. Instead of ears, some use their . . .

Well, let's not begin there. Let's begin by understanding how our own ears work to hear sounds.

The human ear has three parts: the outer ear, the middle ear, and the inner ear. The part of your outer ear that is on the side of your head is called the **pinna.** The pinna catches sound waves, almost as if it were a catcher's mitt. It sends sound waves into the auditory canal and along to the eardrum. Sound waves vibrate, or move quickly, off the walls of the auditory canal. The vibrating action makes some sounds become louder than they were when they first entered the canal.

The eardrum is a thin flap of skin that stretches across the end of the auditory canal. It separates the outer ear and the middle ear. Inside the middle ear are the three smallest bones in our bodies: the **hammer,** the **anvil,** and the **stirrup.** When sound waves make the eardrum vibrate, the vibrations make these bones move. When these bones vibrate, the sound waves are passed on to another thin flap of skin called the oval window. The oval window separates the middle ear and the inner ear.

The middle ear is connected to the back of the throat by the Eustachian tube, which lets air in and out of the middle ear. When you "pop" your ears, this tube suddenly opens.

Hammer

Anvil

Stirrup

Eardrum

In the inner ear is a tube called the **cochlea.** It's about the size of your fingertip, and it has the shape of a snail. The cochlea is filled with fluid called **lymph.** In the middle of the lymph there is a thin strip of skin that is covered by more than two million tiny hairs. Each tiny hair reacts to a particular vibration. When sound waves pass into the inner ear through the oval window, they cause tiny waves, or ripples, in the lymph. When the lymph ripples, these tiny hairs bend. There are nerves along the bottom of these hairs. When the hairs bend, these nerves send messages about sound vibrations to your brain. In a fraction of a second, your brain figures out what the vibrations mean and lets you know what you are hearing. By the time you are an adult, your brain will be able to recognize almost half a million different sounds!

Knowing how people hear will help you understand how some animals hear without using their ears. It all has to do with sound waves and vibrations.

Dolphins

Deep in the ocean, dolphins live in an underwater environment that is often dark and cloudy. Because they cannot depend on their eyesight in these conditions, dolphins have developed an ability to "see" with sound. This ability is called **echolocation.** The first part of the word *echolocation* is *echo*. Can you guess why?

Using echolocation, dolphins use their jaws—not their ears—to feel vibrations. Dolphins have six air sacs underneath their blowholes. By tightening the openings to the air sacs and forcing air through them, dolphins make sounds called echolocation clicks. These clicks are short sound waves.

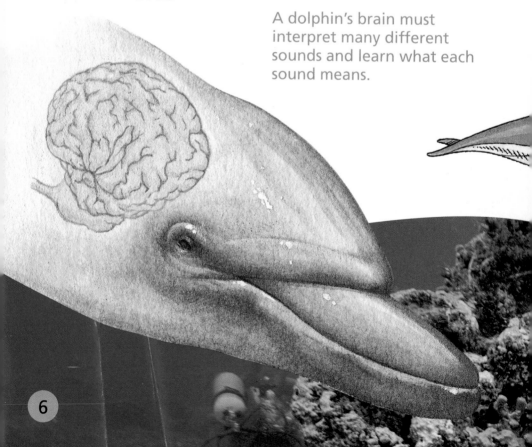

A dolphin's brain must interpret many different sounds and learn what each sound means.

The fat-filled area in the front of a dolphin's head is called the **melon.** The melon focuses, or directs, the clicks as they leave the dolphin's head. The clicks travel out through the water. Some of the clicks echo, or bounce, off objects in the water. (That's where the echo part of the word comes from.) The echoes bounce back toward the dolphin and hit its jaw.

The vibrations travel through the dolphin's lower jaw to its inner ear. Then the vibrations are passed on to the hearing center in the brain.

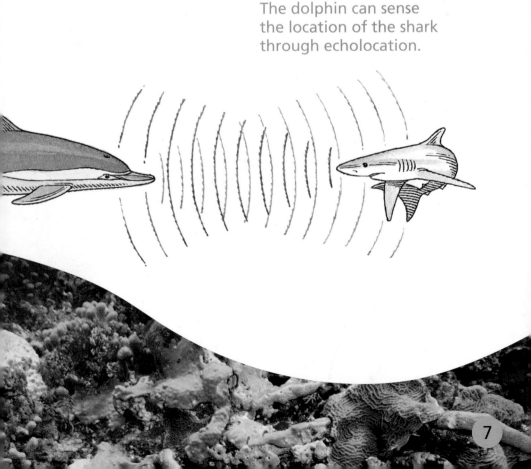

The dolphin can sense the location of the shark through echolocation.

Using echolocation to sense their environments, dolphins create a mental picture of what is in the water around them. They can tell how far away an object is, depending on how quickly or slowly echoes come back. If echoes come back quickly, an object is near. If it takes a while for them to come back, an object is farther away.

Besides figuring out how near or close an object is, echolocation clicks can tell the direction an object is traveling. They can also tell the object's speed, size, and shape.

The killer whale is a type of dolphin.

Dolphins can make hundreds of echolocation clicks in a split second. They can also send out sounds that are powerful enough to stun, or temporarily paralyze, fish. Huge killer whales (which are actually dolphins, not whales) can even stun penguins. This certainly makes food easier to catch!

Humans cannot hear individual echolocation clicks, but we may be able to feel them. If you are ever lucky enough to be in the water with a dolphin that is echolocating, it might be possible for you to feel these clicks passing through the water.

Scientists have done experiments with dolphins to learn about echolocation. They have placed covers over dolphins' eyes and found that the dolphins were still able to find their way to an underwater target. When scientists put soundproof covers over the dolphins' lower jaw, the dolphins were not able to echolocate very successfully.

Even though these studies show that dolphins' eyes are not as important for finding things as their jaws, dolphins actually have very good eyesight. Their eyes move independently, which means that each eye can look at something different at the same time. This ability helps them look out for predators around them. But it is also a problem. Since their eyes are on the sides of their heads, dolphins have trouble seeing things that are straight ahead of them. Echolocation solves that problem.

Just behind their eyes, dolphins have tiny ear holes. Many scientists believe that these ears are only useful for hearing sounds above the surface of the water but not under it.

Dolphins do use their eyes and ears, but it is really their jaws that are most important. Dolphins make and receive other sounds besides clicks. They are very social animals that live in groups called pods. To communicate with members of their own pods, dolphins whistle and make noises. To our ears, these noises sound like squeaks, squeals, and groans. But to other dolphins each sound is a different and important message. Researchers have learned that dolphins can pass along information to other dolphins, such as "I need help" and "There is food here."

Dolphin trainers use whistles and hand signals to communicate with dolphins. The skilled mammals can be trained to leap high out of the water and to do tricks.

Trained dolphins respond to whistles and hand signals when performing tricks.

Dolphins actually call each other by name. Soon after giving birth, a mother dolphin whistles over and over again to her calf. She does this so the calf can find her in a group. The calf's first whistle may be just one long note. The whistle gradually becomes more complicated until it turns into a unique whistle. This new whistle is called a signature whistle. It becomes the dolphin's "name" for the rest of its life.

A dolphin's brain is much larger than the brains of other mammals. Scientists believe that they need large brains to communicate so well and to use complicated echolocation skills.

As you now know, dolphins "hear" very well with body parts other than their ears. Next, you will read about bats. They have huge ears, but they still use echolocation!

Some dolphins communicate through whistles.

Bats

Like dolphins, most bats use echolocation to catch food and to get information about their surroundings. But there are some differences. Bats produce their sound pulses differently from the way that dolphins do.

Dolphins produce sound in their nasal passages. Bats have a **larynx,** or voice box, that produces sound. Some bats send their sounds out of their mouths. Others snort their sound out of their noses. Bats that "call" through their noses have flaps of skin around their noses called **nose leaves.** Nose leaves push the sound waves forward. Nose leaves are handy for bats that carry food in their mouths because the bats are then able to eat and echolocate at the same time! Each kind of bat makes a unique echolocating sound. Just as humans cannot hear dolphins' clicks, we cannot hear most bat sounds either.

Most bats eat insects, but some eat fruit. Usually the insect-eating bats use echolocation. They are the bats with large ears.

Do you remember that our outer ears catch the sound waves around us? Bats' large ears do the same thing—but even better! Our outer ears do not move, but theirs do. Many bats' ears can rotate to catch sound coming from different directions. When they catch sound waves, they direct them to sound-sensitive cells inside their ears. These cells pass along signals to the brain.

As its name indicates, the Egyptian fruit bat (above) eats fruit. Its ears are small because it does not echolocate. The long-eared bat (left) eats insects. Look at the size of its ears!

Have you ever heard the expression "You're as blind as a bat!"? Actually, the expression is misleading because some bats have excellent vision. Bats that eat fruit instead of insects have large, bulging eyes that see very well.

Bats that eat insects need to use echolocation because they hunt at night. At night there is less competition for food and therefore less chance that other animals will hunt the bats themselves! The echolocation method that bats use is very similar to that which dolphins use. As bats cruise through the night sky, they emit, or send out, sound pulses. When the sounds echo back from an object that seems like it might be something to eat, the bat flies in that general direction.

As it flies toward the prey, the bat sends out very short sound pulses—as many as 170 in a second. This is called a feeding buzz. These short sound pulses can detect very tiny objects, such as mosquitoes, moths, or gnats. The pulses also tell how fast and in what direction the objects are moving. A bat's echolocation is precise enough to find even a single strand of hair!

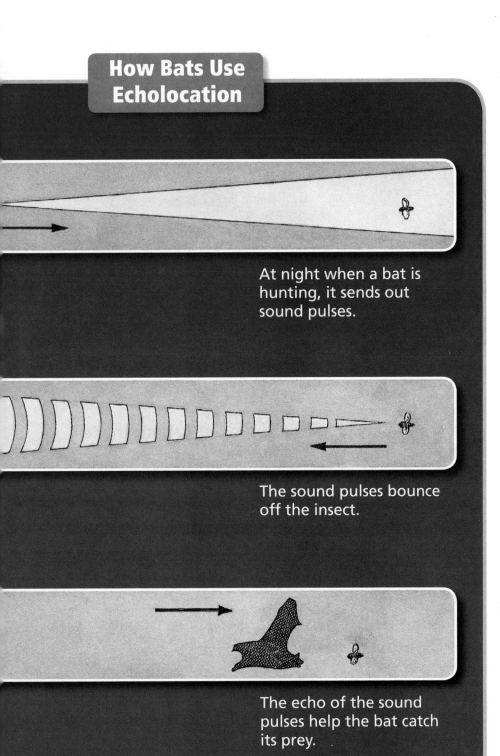

At night when a bat is hunting, it sends out sound pulses.

The sound pulses bounce off the insect.

The echo of the sound pulses help the bat catch its prey.   .

17

Groups of bats often spend their days sleeping in caves.

Many bats love to eat moths! In fact, that's all that some bats will eat. In response to this danger, some kinds of moths have developed their own natural "anti-bat" protection. They have grown fuzzy wings that bats' echolocation pulses won't bounce off of. How effective!

But some bats have found a way around this. They have developed a different kind of echo that can detect fuzzy wings! Maybe fuzzy wings are not so effective after all.

Other moths have ears and are able to hear bats' echolocation pulses. When they hear the pulses, they are warned that a bat is nearby. This warning gives them some time to hide.

One kind of bat, the African heart-nosed bat, can turn off its echolocation pulses and use only its hearing to find prey so that it will not alert animals that it is nearby. Other moths have learned to make sounds that imitate bat noises. When a bat hears this noise, it gets confused and flies right by.

Although we cannot hear most bat pulses, they sound very loud to bats. In fact, they are so loud that bats have to protect themselves from their own sounds. When a bat makes sound pulses, its ear blocks out the noise. As soon as the sound ends, the ear is ready to listen for the returning echo.

Not all the sounds that bats make are for echolocating. Some sounds are made just for communicating with each other. Bats make sounds to defend their own territory and to communicate with their babies. Baby bats live in "nursery caves" with thousands or even millions of other baby bats. Mother bats can locate their own babies by their unique voices.

Many people are afraid of bats. They have heard stories about bats attacking people, but most of these stories are not true. Bats are gentle and shy animals, unless they feel they are being threatened. Bats do a lot of good things for the environment and for us. They spread seeds and pollinate fruits and flowers. They also eat millions of mosquitoes.

This is a short-tailed leaf-nosed bat, named for the shape of its nose.

Not many animals have the ability to echolocate. The shrew, a mouselike mammal, is one of the few animals that echolocate to discover information about its surroundings. Its method of echolocation is not nearly as advanced as that of the dolphin or the bat. Like dolphins, some species of shrews emit clicks. Their clicks help them find worms and insects in the dark.

Next time you are riding in a car or on the school bus, close your eyes and try to imagine that you are a dolphin swimming in a dark ocean or a bat flying through a forest at midnight. Try to "see" a mental picture of your surroundings, using only your sense of hearing. What are you passing on your right? On your left? Is something in front of you? Is something coming toward you?

Wouldn't echolocation clicks come in handy?

Shrews are very small and weigh about as much as a nickel.

Now Try This

EXPERIMENT WITH SOUND!

As you have read, dolphins make sound waves. They use echolocation clicks to navigate and to find food. As you also know, dolphins make and receive other sounds, such as whistles, that sound like squeaks to our ears.

High sounds have fast vibrations, and low sounds have slow vibrations. Try demonstrating this with a piece of rope. If you hold one end of the rope and a friend holds the other, you can practice making fast and slow waves, or vibrations. With a flick of your wrist, you can make a long, slow wave. If you move your hand faster, you can make shorter, faster waves. Short, fast sound waves make higher sounds, or pitches, than longer, slower sound waves.

Try experimenting with sound waves by making high and low pitches!

Moving your hand slower makes longer waves.

Moving your hand faster makes shorter waves.

1 Gather several glasses of the same size and line them up on a table. Starting with the glass on the right, fill it with about half an inch of water. Move down the line filling each glass with a little more water. You should be able to see that each glass has more water in it than the glass to its right.

2 With a piece of silverware, lightly tap the glass to hear a sound. As you move down the line tapping each glass, notice how the pitch of the sound changes. Does the pitch sound high or low? Does that mean that the sound wave is short and fast or long and slow?

3 Think about the vibrations you and a friend can create with a rope. On a piece of paper, draw a line showing what the sound wave coming from each glass might look like. Do the waves in your lines get longer or shorter as the pitch gets lower?

Glossary

anvil *n.* the central bone of three tiny bones in the middle ear.

cochlea *n.* a spiral-shaped tube in the inner ear.

echolocation *n.* a method of finding objects by using sound waves and vibrations.

hammer *n.* the outermost bone of three tiny bones in the middle ear.

larynx *n.* voice box.

lymph *n.* the fluid in the cochlea.

melon *n.* the fat-filled area in the front of a dolphin's head that focuses the echolocation clicks as they leave the dolphin's head.

nose leaves *n.* the flaps of skin on a bat's nose that direct sound forward.

pinna *n.* the skin-covered outer part of an ear.

stirrup *n.* the innermost of three tiny bones in the middle ear.